T0113596

The Wonderful and Great Power of

GOD

27 Years of Sobriety

*2 Corinthians 5:17 NIV Therefore, if anyone
is in Christ, he is a new creation; the old has
gone, the new has come.*

Brenda A Merritt

authorHOUSE®

AuthorHouse™
1663 Liberty Drive
Bloomington, IN 47403
www.authorhouse.com
Phone: 833-262-8899

© 2021 Brenda A Merritt. All rights reserved.

No part of this book may be reproduced, stored in a retrieval system, or
transmitted by any means without the written permission of the author.

Published by AuthorHouse 01/12/2022

ISBN: 978-1-6655-4847-2 (sc)
ISBN: 978-1-6655-4846-5 (e)

Library of Congress Control Number: 2022900408

Print information available on the last page.

Any people depicted in stock imagery provided by Getty Images are models,
and such images are being used for illustrative purposes only.
Certain stock imagery © Getty Images.

This book is printed on acid-free paper.

Because of the dynamic nature of the Internet, any web addresses or
links contained in this book may have changed since publication and
may no longer be valid. The views expressed in this work are solely those
of the author and do not necessarily reflect the views of the publisher,
and the publisher hereby disclaims any responsibility for them.

Scripture quotations marked NKJV are taken from the
New King James Version. Copyright © 1982 by Thomas
Nelson, Inc. Used by permission. All rights reserved.

Scripture quotations marked KJV are from the Holy Bible,
King James Version (Authorized Version). First published
in 1611. Quoted from the KJV Classic Reference Bible,
Copyright © 1983 by The Zondervan Corporation.

Scripture quotations marked NIV are taken from the Holy
Bible, New International Version®. NIV®. Copyright ©
1973, 1978, 1984 by International Bible Society. Used by
permission of Zondervan. All rights reserved. [Biblica]

CONTENTS

DEDICATIONS

To: My four beautiful children and their children

As well as the Seven that went to Heaven

To: The still suffering Alcoholic and Addicts

To: Those who are suffering from Mental Illness because of Abuse or for whatever the reasons.

Remember, The same cracker different wrapper.

ACKNOWLEDGEMENTS

First and foremost, Thanks to My Loving God, whom I choose to call, God. You are the Greatest Father of all.

To my best friend Ray Ray (RIH) you WERE AND STILL IS an awesome INSPIRATIONAL BEING IN MY LIFE. Thank You from THE deeper than the DEEPEST PART OF my Heart.

To my eldest son, Mike who did in fact purchase me a laptop. It was many years ago, but the time is now.

God's time. He alone has given me THE ABILITY TO complete my Autobiography in a series.

To my manager: Gee along with my Supervisor Ray Ray. Words can't express the wonderful and great spiritual connection that we endured the first time we met. I love the both of you along with their family.

Of course, there were many others who decided to move on with their lives. You will be forever appreciated.

THE PURPOSE FOR WRITING THIS BOOK

First of all, God gave me the concept of writing my testimony. He ordered my desire to carry His message concerning mental illness/substance abuse. Only in His order and time for me has He guided me to give back to the community in which much was taken.

He had given me the knowledge to pass the test of the Fundamentals of Substance Abuse Class (F.O.S.A.C.) with rainbow colors. However; I was unable to practice as a Licensed Certified Counselor because of a previous felony charge that consisted of a bodily harm. Which was never the whole truth so help me God.

That law led me to continue praying for God to open a different door. "Behold I stand at the door, and knock: if any man hear my voice, and open the door, I will come to him, and will sup with him, and he with me".

Revelation 3:20

Because, one thing is certain, God hadn't brought me that far too just leave me back then.

He HAS GIVEN me THE BEST DAYS OF MY LIFE. I AM SO HAPPY AND ME.

Today I can tell my testimony based on the truth about what is bound to happen if we continue to allow ourselves to be abused by others as well as ourselves.

There's proof that we are unique in our own way, however it's also true that addicts have the same similarities in personality and we hold a common bond. It's just the situations that may vary.

God's mission is geared for me to elaborate on the core of my mental disorder and substance abuse. After admitting there is a problem, then we can chose to be part of God's solution for it all. I'm hoping to touch at least one person's heart, as I reflect on God's messages throughout this entire book. May He have the Victory, Glory, and Honor forever and ALWAYS.

He showed me that the only way to effective living is for me to follow His instructions. He is the truth and the BEST life at such a time like this, always was and will always be.

As I repeat the words that God whispers in my ears. Please know that His purpose is not for me to point my finger at anyone for their DIFFERENT choices THAT I may not

AGREE WITH. Because I'll find 3 more fingers pointing back at me.

I have learned that no one is responsible for the actions I made or continue to make. I did in fact choose to dedicate 90 percent of my participation to the games.

Plus, I had to realize that my deceptions of others stems from within self. In which there lies a desire to change.

God carried me through many trials and tribulations in order for me to be the Survivor that I am. He's strengthening me to tell it all over the world. Believe that, because as we see what He does for others, He will do for me and you AS WELL. Thank Him in advance, better yet we can speak it into existence.

My desire is to express my deepest sympathy, remorse, and gratitude that led to my horrific beginning, Perhaps it all brought me through my despair that ended in a wonderful and great life. Today I will start each day as a new beginning.

The names have been changed to
protect the privacy of others.

ABOUT THE AUTHOR

Brenda Merritt, the author, was born to my parents. Vernatine Merritt and Rayfield Brown (May the both of them Rest in heaven). I was also born and raised in Milwaukee, Wisconsin.

"I must admit that I do in fact have a series of mental health disorders which stemmed from an abusive dysfunctional upbringing and I heard that I inherited other issues. I say that out of all honesty, not to blame anyone".

I was diagnosed BY MEN with Attention Deficit Hyperactivity Disorder (A D H D), Bi-Polar, and Chronic Depression. I also experience physical damage to my back, HEAD and sciatica nerve. BOTTOM LINE IS THAT MY SPINE IS DAMAGED.

Throughout my life I was physically abused in the worst manner.

Traumatized, Dramatized, Victimized and Brutalized. Beginning at age five to age thirty-five.

At this time, I have Osteoporosis and Arthritis throughout my body. For Therapy I use many body braces, MEDICATION THAT I NO LONGER ABUSE, DANCING, AND Yoga. This therapy needs to be inactive daily. I have decided to become a pescatarian, AS WELL AS to eliminate dairy products. It's not a diet, just a healthy way of eating.

Well readers I have been writing since I was a little girl, age 7. I started out with a diary, the place where I would write out all the sick secrets that surrounded my life on a regular basis. Therefore, I have many books that are in the making to look forward too.

However, today I am at the end of my twenty ninth year of Sobriety. As I look back on the many years that I've attempted to complete one of my books, I had realized my child within was terribly afraid to reveal the truth of the abusive situations that occurred. Even though my adult self is now saying: "Discussing these matters could very well set you free for the rest of my life".

I asked myself. "What are you afraid of Brenda Anne, Brenly, Bree Bree or Benna?" ... Or whatever my name is. Lol

On the real tip though, I may have split personalities after all. I'll admit 70% of the times, I'm Brenda

One of the reasons is that unlike the majority of the students, my ability to focus in a classroom setting was obsolete in my confused mind. Secondly are about how my significant others would judge me. Yes, them. Not God. Even though, The Bible says: he that is without sin among you, let him first cast a stone at her". John 8:7 KJV. Therefore, how much power are you going to give those people?

Age 7 years old until this time I have written so many journals reflecting on the same type of abusive situations that occurred in my life. I found myself working on different ones in order to run from one to another. Some circumstances are hurtful.

I had rather stayed in and out of circles within a vicious cycle. As you see I couldn't figure out how to go any further. I found myself in a big ball of confusion.

But low and behold the books are about to give birth. One at a time. YESSSSSSSSS

Now it's time for me to come correct. I am now ready to write my story about my twenty-nine years of Sobriety.

I'm starting from the beginning of the last time that I hit rock bottom. Ending in an order to be in this present time. To the best of my ability.

I had to decide to surrender all.

Please hear what I cannot say:
This is an old poem that I had attempted to revise.

Try not to be fooled by me,

Because, on my face is a mask, many masks, masks that

I'm ashamed to take off,

HOWEVER, trust me, none of them are me, To pretend is a learned behavior for me,

So, you can't believe me sometimes. For God's sake don't.

I may give you the wrong impression sometimes. So, you won't know the pain from my tears inside. If you laugh at me, you will kill me.

The name of my game is I'm cool, calm and collected. That I'm in control. But for real I'm disconnected

So no, you NEED NOT TO trust me.

My appearance may look genuine, or even authentic. THOUGH YOU CAN BELIEVE Underneath there's the mask, different kinds

THEY ARE CONFUSED, ABUSED AND USED. Sort of sick My heart is SO VERY broken, will it ever be a love token I JUST ASKED.

LIKE THAT

That's Okay you will not worry ABOUT ME, I'M NOBODY, For God's sake somethings I CAN'T SAY.

not YET.

PROLOGUE

To the people who do not know my entire life story yet choose to judge me for my past negative choices, please read this book, along with others in the making. It may save your life or the life of a loved one.

If you can sit around and communicate my faults with other listeners. I want to challenge you to find out what really happened in my life. What caused this USED TO BE human being to act out like a mental ill patient.

Today the extra ordinary storms have seemed to calm down in my life. Perhaps, I know now that my perception on life and the people therein had to change. In an order to keep my sanity as I receive God's Blessings:

Believing and Trusting in His Holy name.

Going out on Faith as small as a mustard seed. May you find Him today because tomorrow isn't promised.

Therefore, be in it to win it! Get in where you fit in. For me, I TRY THE STRAIGHT AND NARROW ROAD

SOMETIMES. OTHER TIMES I'M STRADDLING THE FENCE, But I BEWARE AND STAY WOKE.

I can finally see peace in my valley. And yes, I am still in the valley.

Now that I know for a fact that I am a child of God.

Thanks to The Lord Jesus Christ I can breathe again. His wonderful mighty power has allowed me to grow and glow.

I can do all things through Christ who strengthen me. Philippians 4:13 NKJV

I can rebuke the evil one and all its weak followers in the mightiest way. I put on my Armor of God and fight for the rights that I am entitled to.

There is the God in me. He is standing at His throne welcoming me with strong hands and powerful Agape love and unspeakable joy. I AM HAPPY today. Still human, but HAPPY about my place of being. I can't explain how lovable God is. It's beyond my understanding.

CHAPTER 1

The Road Where My Life Was Devastating

It was 1991 when I, at age thirty-five, was at the highest peck of my tolerance for drugs. They just wouldn't get me high any longer. However, my drug of choice was beer.

Even though cocaine and heroin were secondary to me, I've found that a drug, is a drug is a drug. That even means weed. It's a drug, so all of you who use it, need to understand that reality, instead of criticizing others who are entitled to choose differently.

That devastating time of my life when I hit rock bottom was actually the worst experience of my thirty-five years of living.

During this time in my life, I was still on parole with the Federal government for credit card fraud. The outpatient substance abuse treatment was mandatory. I was ordered to attend Wisconsin Correctional Services (W C S), where

I would maintain a psychiatrist. His name was Dr. Deorbit. He prescribed lots of psychotic medicines that were not good for me. I complained over and over again to no avail. So, I continued to follow the rules and regulations which were to give the medications time to work.

After being clean for six months, I relapsed on my drug of choice alcohol. I found out quickly that that wasn't the answer. Soon after, I topped mixing that medicine with beer. However, I noticed that would take me to a different place where I didn't want to be. I had started hallucinating by hearing vicious voices.

I would pray and discuss all that was going on with me to a dear friend named Veverly, and foremost I would light candles and pray to Jesus. I remember being fully aware of everything that had taken place around those times my troubled life. My parole officer became concerned. I told her all that was going down and told her the truth about how I wasn't having the best response to that medicine. Over and over again. Seriously. I pleaded I even suggested if I could try something different. She insisted that I continue to take those particular pills and even said that if I refused, it would be a violation of my parole. So I kept taking for a little while longer without drinking. I was so damn terrified and very concerned about what was taking place in my head. I thought that if I didn't mix the medicine my thoughts would change. Which was the wrong answer, So I continued to complain and pray for someone to help me.

I was determined to get off that medicine. even if it meant for my five-year stayed sentence from the federal credit card fraud charge that I was serving, would be revoked My court papers read, "United States of America vs, Brenda Merritt". As if I were a menace to society.

I had begun to feel very depressed again. It was hard as hell to figure out how I would handle that situation, though finally deciding to call one of my brothers was a possibility. His name is Free. I called him on the phone, explained what was going on with me and how I was hallucinating. He came over to the beautiful house on Thirty-Eightht where my three children and I were residing. We agreed that I needed to go to the hospital. After being admitted, the doctors wouldn't change anything. I was instructed to consult with my parole officer. They did admit me until that action would take place. My children went to be with my mother until further notice.

I felt so trapped and miserable about the whole situation, but giving up was not an option, because something inside me was driving me to get help. There was a huge desire within my soul to fight my battle, even though I found out that battle was not mine, it belonged to the Lord. So, I called my parole officer once again to request further assistance. Previously, I'd told her about hearing voices telling me to cut my kids" heads off and then mine. heads off and then mine.

Eventually, she came to the hospital and ordered me to report back to the halfway house for a certain length of time. I had been ordered to reside there after being released from the House of Correction many times before. The staff knew me very well.

Ever been excited to go to a halfway house?

After I was released from that hospital, I went home to pack up. I put my furniture into a storage. I explained as much as I could to my children. I hugged my most precious children goodbye, and headed out. Something inside of me was like, oh my God, I felt sadness and gladness all at the same time, However, I cried a river for several years afterward. But, my mission was to get the necessary help so that I wouldn't continue to treat myself or my precious children unhealthy.

As soon as I entered the halfway house, my guardian angel, Barb, insisted that I was to be admitted back to the Mental Health Complex to have an evaluation. My behavior was strange and out of ordinary. After she had taken all the necessary steps for me to return to the hospital. My original Doctor, whom I had seen there several times before, immediately discontinued the entire list of those psychotic medications which were not helping me but instead harming me. He prescribed one pill for me for my insomnia.

He released me a few days later after seeing a normal response of stability.

About two days after I returned to the halfway house, it was time for me to meet with my case manager, Mrs. Tall. She was very familiar with me as well. I mentioned to her my main short-term goal, which was to enroll into a counseling program together with my children. My mission was to inform them of what had truly happened to their mother and what had driven me to maintain my dysfunctional lifestyle. I wanted them to know that I loved them dearly and that I didn't mean any harm.

I wanted to apologize. In which the staff at the Halfway House agreed to allow that service to take place.

However, as the meeting continued, Mrs. Tall was concerned about why this particular guy, would come to visit me each time that I went back and forth to that halfway house. I made it my business to express the things that I had experienced in my childhood with the guy.

God led me to honestly tell her about my sick secrets. We had the best conversation ever. It seemed to have touched her in a valuable at such a time like that. However, after the conversation, she felt the need to report some of the things that I had mentioned to her.

CHAPTER 2

The Lane Where I Went Through Incarceration Again

As time passed, my children knew that they wouldn't see me for a while, but there were no worries because I told them that I was a survivor So even though I admitted to neglecting them, it didn't make my actions right. I was dead wrong, and I made sure to tell them that. Soon after it was time for the misery to end and I swore on my life to become better. I meant that on everything I loved. I had surrendered to God and asked him to let His will be done with my self-destructive life, I asked Him to give me the strength to carry it out. I am proud to say that He did just that and more.

1992, my parole officer revoked me, and I had to go to prison for five years. I did not blame her for my bad choice that I had in fact act out, but what puzzled me was why she didn't tell the whole story.

What happened to me was never mentioned throughout the entire trail. I became the fall guy.

I was charged with a bodily harm crime which carried a three-year sentence, the judge ordered for the state time to run concurrent to the federal sentence, meaning I would complete the state time while in the federal prison because I owed them five years.

It was a wrap. Thank God.

The nearest federal prison was The Women's Correctional Facility, located in Lexington, Kentucky. I would be unable to see my children. They wouldn't be able to visit. It was too far, My journey to get to my destination was first to Waukesha federal county Jail, which I called the "old-school jail". That term was because it still had the big heavyduty bars that the officers would slam on a daily basis. That sound would make my whole-body tremble. I was like Hell They were bogus for that. That noise stayed in my head for many years after leaving the facility.

It was the place where the federal inmates were housed until their next destination. I had come across many of the big ballers and shot callers. Yes, they used to be big dough wheels that had been busted for sailing illegal drugs charges which consisted of a lot of money. I was just grateful in a sense for my short five years, because they were facing a life sentence, behind bars. That was way over my head. There were also some of the ringleaders of the dope game, along with their workers. I remembered the days when they all were doing it big.

Anyway, I didn't communicate too much with anyone actually, I was writing a book that I titled Foxy, anovel about the fast track. It wasn't long before the feds came to take us to the next stop, which was the Metropolitan Correctional Center (MCC) in Chicago, a federal prison. We were housed on the thirteenth floor, which was very overcrowded. But just like a lot of the other jails, the process was the same. After the booking, we had to be stripped of all clothing, they would check our hair, instruct us tosquat, cough, bend over to spread our cheeks and open our mouths, then we would put on our jail attire. They would also put our personal belongings in a safe locker.

I would only chat with a few of the ladies. I knew better than to get too friendly with certain ones. There was nothing new about doing time in those jails. The women along with the Officers were two faced drama queens and kings, so I chilled most of the time. It was only another brief layover. There were a lot of confrontations on a regular basis at that particular jail. My name wasn't in any of that mess.

A matter of fact I had never been so serious about striving to get to an unlimited unconditional love in my new life. I was at a turning point that I heard in the lyrics of a song. Though, I never knew what the guy was meaning in what he was singing. Actually, I didn't even like the song. Well, back then I was young and full of calm. Very naïve. However, I was truly ready to change my whole perspective on my life. God had given me a wakeup call and I chose to take advantage of it. Although; after being so dysfunctional, and broken for what seemed like a thousand years, made that change very complicated to achieve. However, there wasn't anything too big for God. The one that I had finally decided to follow. Especially after seeing all else had failed.

Surprisingly, one early morning the feds came to pick us up to take us to Lexington Federal Institution. Their rule was that they didn't want us to know the exact departure date nor time, which was in an order to prevent the possibility of the inmates escaping.

After that long ass process. It must have been at least ten of us loading up on the Prison Bus.

I was fortunate to have the ability to sit by the window in deep thought. Just reflecting on what was bound to take place in my life. I knew that it was going to be whatever I made of it. I noticed the beauty of the sceneries of the fields and trees which were filled with snow, while others had frozen ice on them.

For most of the ride my spirit was well. I knew I was on the road to rehabilitation. I was so hungry to go to any length to get it. And that that's just what I did and is continuing to do today.

I prayed all the way.

We stopped at Juliet County jail for a layover. We spent the night there, as usual the capacity was above its means, so we had to sleep on the floor. The best part of that layover was we only stayed for one night and after we left from there it was the last jail before our destination. So, we stopped at Mickey Ds for breakfast, lunch then dinner at the appointed times. Yes, with hand cuffs and shackles around our ankles. Along with chains from waist to waist that connected us all together … we would be removed from the bus one by one. One step at a time. I was thinking like, coldblooded, whatever y'all. I felt like a toddler who could only take baby steps. Those baby steps hurtled badly as we walked.

Those officers got on my damn nerves. They were treating us as if we were Solders in the Army. Putting us in a single file. I remember the parents grabbing a hold on their children as they realized our situation.

We were there within two days. Traveling through the out shirts of Lexington was a beautiful sight to see. I had the opportunity to see why it was called the land of the Blue Grass. The grass was amazingly so deep green until it looked blue. It was awesome. Seemed like God had already started showing me how He was going to make my negative out of a positive situation. All I needed to do was to follow through.

There the humongous building was in the middle of many acres of land. It was a long road that led us to the actual prison ground. The building itself was huge, there was a name on a large sign that says; The Federal Medical Center.

I heard it housed at least 1,500 inmates in which at that particular time it was women only.

Man, I felt butterflies going around in my stomach, because what I had seen seemed to be a little spooky to me; and my curiosity didn't make anything any better. So ok, once again we get off the bus to form a single line. Bear with me as I describe this prison site to the very best of my ability. It's so much.

The main gate opened as we entered the front of building. We were ordered to walk down a long narrow walk way that led us to the inside of the booking area. Which was also right next to the prison yard. There were plenty gay chicks standing along the short-gated brick wall, who were checking us out as we slowly kept in step with one another. They were whistling at us and even choosing which one of us that they wanted. Now that was different as well as scary. Actually, most of the procedure was different. It was my first-time experiencing life in a Federal Prison. We were really the walking living dead.

In the processing room things were the same as the other facilities such as finger prints, mug(photos) shots and the checking of the body and hair. The other thing different was that we did take a shower before leaving from the booking department.

The guards gave us a couple settings of clothing, personal needs and towels. Another important thing that they had given to each one of us was a Rule and Regulations booklet. It was the introduction to the prison. Right away I noticed the everyday stand up at the door 4:00pm count. Plus, a ten-minute movement stop. Meaning every ten minutes to an hour we had to be at our destination. At certain hours.

After we were dressed, they directed us to our assigned unit. For me and a few others ladies were taken to a unit with many different rooms. We were housed in a room which had eight beds and the lockers were in there as well. The Officers called it an eight-man room.

Though, it depended on the longevity that an inmate had before they could be moved to a 1or 2-man room. First come, first moved to a smaller room.

Well, it had taken me a long time to adjust to a room like that.

In an order to cope, I prayed regularly.

I did not like it there. So, I decided to just cry until I would get tired. Day in day out. Week after week. Month after month. In the meantime. Off and on. Trust me I cried for a whole year before I decided or realized that I wasn't running anything. My pity potty was over, That I was there.

As a result of all the stress I caused myself. My menstruation came down which seemed to have had an endless flow. In reality I was just straight up depressed and stressed in the hell out!

Wasn't too much of anything that I could do about it. Plus, the Unit Attendant said that there was a long wait to see the doctor for the new comers. Though there was hope, because some of the ladies told me that he would eventually call sooner than later. That I would get a full physical.

In the meantime, I was assigned to work on the dorm, that job paid like twenty-five cent an hour, though after meeting my case manager she reassured me that I wouldn't be working there long. However, she also told me that I had to do five years, in which I refused to claim. Day in and day out I kept waiting to wake up out of the nightmare that I was stuck in. But yet instead reality kept kicking in and I was really there. My release date was February 05, 1995. My counselor had also given me a long list of things to get involved with.

What really caught my eye was an Inpatient Twelve Month Substance Abuse Program. That along was the greatest option that I had encountered since I had been there. I was excited about going to the orientation.

Be mindful that my menstruation was still at flow.

On the appointed time and day, there were many ladies going to room 101 where we were introduced to The Substance Abuse Program. It had lasted a good hour. The ones, who wanted to attend the program, stayed and filled out some forms. Before we left the room the Facilitator let us know if were accepted the Officer would notify us with the start date. Sure, enough I was accepted. The program was arranged to be held in a building that set outside from the main buildings. Up on a hill right off the huge track and field. The gate extended all the way around the entire prison. Yep, with the bob wire. It was the one that

I saw as we were driving up Leestown Rd. I just While we were approaching the Prison, I had noticed it and figured it was just some old building. That had closed down. For one thing it looked secluded.

The main building had the dining area, library, infirmary, auditorium, commissary, gym, classrooms, a chapel with the church area, and just many other business offices.

Reflection: There it was a real prison. I found out a little more history about the place. It used to be an Inpatient Drug Rehabilitation Facility for the rich and famous people only. They went there for whatever met their needs.

They had changed it over to a male only prison at one time.

Next it went co-ed meaning men and women together. That most defiantly didn't work out.

One thing for sure it was a lot different from the State Penitentiary. (Though, I had never been ordered to go there). From this point on I will be reflecting on some of my experiences that had taken place in the Prison.

We were able to order a certain amount of our own clothes, called it a Box. We could go to the movies every weekend, walk the track, just did the darn thing. I was like … YES!

A matter of fact going to prison saved my life; instead of being arrested I was rescued. I actually felt like it was a God thing that I was supposed to be there in order to get a chance at true living, real life, a natural high and to become the women that I was meant to be. Far as my child with-in, she was only a part of me.

A couple of months had passed and my menstruation was still flowing so I decided to take the situation to a prayer meeting that some of us had started. We would meet at the end of the hallway on the floor where the majority of us were housed. There was an elder lady in our circle who claimed to be a Prophet. She prayed for me referring to the story in the Holy Bible, about a woman who also had an on-going flow, and was healed by Jesus. A different lady recited Matthew 18: 19-20. As a result of that study, 3 days later the flow had come to a complete stop. I couldn't take it. But, my first impose was to tell the whole world about that miraculous testimony. I just went to several different people telling them about how God had delivered me. However, when I went to tell the Prophet the results and thanked her. We were all excited! But the next thing you know, she asked me to buy her a pack of cigarettes. ☹ I felt sad after that because I had already heard through the grape vine that those type of women were all about money. Preaching and Praying for a profit. All along they had alternative motives and hidden agendas. However, she got the cigarettes and continued to ask for other items as well. That was a red flag for me to turn in the other direction whenever I would see her coming my way.

Finally. I was moved to the new unit where the program would soon resume. There was so much joy and excitement in my heart.

I was housed in a two-man room. My first roommate and I were really cool. Thank God.

As time went on and I started meeting different ladies, some of them were gay, though normally they were cool to communicate with and respected the fact that all of us wasn't down with the same ole' same ole' game.

However, I had noticed a chick that favored Wonderful, (my x pimp), she was attracted to me and didn't care what anyone said. She was informed about how I wasn't gay but insisted on getting my attention. She stayed over in the population area. Which was the main place that all of the women who were not in the program were housed. It was like the majority of the time that I would go over to the cafeteria or the other functions, we would run into one another. She would just stand against the wall with one of her legs up. She would do a little cool pose' and stare at me.

I wanted to ask her if I could have my face back.

Eventually she caught my attention to the point where I found myself thinking about changing my preference for man, to a woman.

But yet instead with that thought. I checked myself with the quickness. That thought was way out there to me ... Therefore, some of the ladies and I got together and prayed ... a lot, though my feelings didn't change right away. I just decided to do what I knew was right anyway. It wasn't about a temporally good feeling for me anymore.

Every day, we would go the cafeteria to at least have three meals. Some of the times we would find those plastic gloves in our soup. Which was the reason why some of us who could afford to buy our own food would stay on the unit to cook. Our specialty was to make enchiladas, by putting them on the radiator. It was our only means to make warm food. Unfortunately, I didn't have too much cash around that time. Therefore, most of the times I had no other choice except to depend on what was being served in the cafeteria.

For me, it was whatever the situation was about, being grateful was in my survival kit. I just kept a positive outlook and hoped for the best. And things did eventually get better for me.

On certain days I would have a meeting with my counselor and also a case manager. At one of those meetings, they informed me about a new position that hired me. My first day started immediately. It was called Unicor. A place which consisted of making several army equipment. A better paying job and the highest paying job at the Prison. For the Inmates. One dollar an hour!

Wasn't that it! I worked on the line soldering, though soon after I had learned my supervisor hired me to be her secretary. Which enabled me to get a raise.

Everything was going in my favor except I hardly ever received mail. Something that was very essential to an inmate. I used to go to mail call hoping to hear from somebody, but to no avail. Every blue moon, my mom would send me a money order from herself and my eldest son. Which was good looking out, though I would only get a receipt. My feelings would hurt sadly, because I didn't get any letters with encouraging words. Nor did I know how my children were doing, Eventually, I just stopped going to mail call. If by chance something would come through, the Officer would put our name on a broad that was hanging on a wall by the front desk, to inform us about any notices including mail. Rarely was my name on the board. I learned to start saying: So, what to myself!

My agenda was to be at work at from 8-12 then program from 1-4 which was good for me. For recreation I would walk the track and attend many inspirational classes. My weekends were spent with hours of studying and Church on Sundays.

I had made up my mind to put forth my greatest effort into the process of the Program, allowing God's will to be done in all my ways one day at a time.

That included for me to first be prayerful. Specifying for Him to bridle my tongue. Therefore, the possibility for me to be as honest, open and willing would be fulfilled. I had also realized that in order to be successful in The Program that I would receive all the qualities from what I put into it and I couldn't keep what I had unless I would give it away. Meaning to share all of my experiences and what I had learned, as well as discussing the benefits of the program. On the other hand, being cautious about who we befriended and even mindful of the places that I chose to go.

So therefore, I had one associate, someone that I trusted. She was from Chicago.

Right away, there went a rumor going around saying that we were dating. The both of us knew what time that was. Neither one of us went that way; people just had to forever keep up mess. She was cool as all get up and nice looking, but I was really attracted to her spirituality. She had a fantastic personality. Just like a lot of us she had been through many trials and tribulations which built her muscle to become the person that she truly was. For me, I was still stuck on my feelings for Miss. Wonderful. However, the best thing about that was because I was fully aware of those feelings and was definitely committed to be a part of the solution. Yeah, that attraction was something else. Though I handled it very good and did not give it any power over what my purpose stood for.

My desire to stop smoking came before I had joined a nonsmoking class. My instructor said that I had to stop hanging around those people and the places which involved cigarettes, that it was triggers. So there is, in fact, footsteps to take before the end. So, I prayed and prayed every time that desire to smoke came about. I'll never forget the last day was when one morning I had went to the smoke room to smoke and I had taken my first but last pull from a cigarette because that thing liked to choke me to death. After putting it down, it's been twenty-nine years. I'm still smoke free. Glory to God.

All of my five senses that had been affected by the drug nicotine, had been redeemed. My food tasted so good. That was another result of doing the right thing. However, yes, I gained weight like crazy, but lost it after taking control of my appetite. Keeping myself busy doing positive things helped me to become a better person.

The first phase of the program was based on the first of the twelve steps.

My counselor and I discussed some very valuable information. I cried every day that I needed too, at work or where ever it didn't matter. I cried. Basically, it was because I had suppressed so many feelings for such a long time.

I had started having sleepless nights, which made my days miserable. Several of the ladies and I had taken the situation to God in prayer and one night my answer was revealed. The Lord said that I needed to talk with someone about the secrets that had kept me in bondage for many years. So, later on in that following evening I immediately discussed it with my counselor. She was very supportive and had given me some positive feedback. It was like I had been waiting to exhale. Literally.

Now remember every situation was only as powerful as we allowed it to be. With that notion, perhaps that's why my prison experience worked out as a great thing for me. My rude awakenings turned into spiritual ones.

Had I not been so very hungry for a change to come into my life, there would not have been any growth or peace. For which I am grateful.

I remember being so full of God's blessings that I didn't have room for more. That was when I realized what it meant when I had read in the Bible where one of His disciples speaks about how the Lord will open up the window and pour you out Blessings that you won't have room for any more.

That it wasn't about receiving a muti-million-dollar check, the Blessings were priceless. Money could not have bought my spirituality or God's supernatural promises.

So many positive things started happening in all areas of my life while I was in Prison. Especially after I was Baptized.

Just to name a few more:

1. I was chosen to attend a week end Seminar that was being held in the main building in the Chapel. I was just sitting there glancing around at all the beautiful things and human beings that were in that huge room. There had to be more than a hundred people altogether. A lot of them were Christians from different Ministries, who volunteered to come to the prison with Hopes

to save lives. The Holy Spirit was in that Chapel. Because, at one of the times that we were praying. Suddenly, the best feeling ever had entered my gut in the center of my stomach. I mean I felt something so wonderful that I hadn't ever experienced in my whole entire life, it aroused in the center of my stomach but quickly disappeared, something had touched me, it was amazing, awesome, and it was love. And it all came from God. All I could do was cry, cried tears of unspeakable joy and I was so speechless. I thought to myself … wow wee … what the world was that … However, the entire Seminar was designed with many classes fulfilled with a number of fantastic activities that were all spiritual based.

2. Another time was when I started singing with the choir. Our rehearsals were awesome. The choir director was instructing each of us to sing a verse or two. It was to my surprise that I did very well when she called on me. I mean I used to sing when I was a little girl. But after I started smoking weed and cigarettes. I lost my gift to sing. And no, it wasn't as if I could sing like a bird. I just had a lovely small voice that God had Blessed me with to serve His purpose.

Every Sunday we would sing our hearts out to a chapel filled with ladies who were seeking strength from God. By doing so my mind became more God like, something I truly wanted and needed.

3. When the time came for the Anniversary of the Substance Abuse Program. They needed an Emcee speaker. The Staff along with the two hundred participants voted for that person. That person was me; they had chosen me to be that speaker. That was an awesome choice. I also played like 3 other parts of the Ceremony.

4. Another great one was accomplishing my GED. All in all, I had accomplished like sixteen different certificates at that Prison.

Certificate of Achievement

This Certifies that

Brenda Merritt

has completed the

Horizon House Program

Given on *October 29, 1990* in Milwaukee, Wisconsin

President — Board of Directors

Director

Program Coordinator

24

C E R T I F I C A T E   O F

Baptism — symbolizes
confession of faith in Christ
adoption into the family of God
commissioned for service

In harmony with our Lord's command, **BRENDA MERRITT**

was baptized at **Lexington, Ky.** on the **27th** day of **June** , 19 **92**

and received into the **Lima Drive** Seventh-day Adventist Church

of the **South Central** Conference on the **27th** day of **June** , 19 **92**

V.E. White, Sr.   _Sis. M.J. Brown_
Officiating Minister   Church Clerk

CERTIFICATE OF ACHIEVEMENT

This certifies that

Brenda Anne Merritt

Successfully Completed the Cognitive Thinking: **Social Survival Skills Course**

with 45 hours

This certificate is hereby issued this **6th** *day of* **December 1993**

Supervisor of Education

Program Coordinator

26

All is well, it's getting better and the best is yet to come.

TRUST IN THE PROCESS
FOURTH ANNIVERSARY CELEBRATION
AUGUST 27, 1993

Welcome . . . . *B. Merritt

Invocation. . . . . A. Church, Chaplain

Always Tomorrow . . . . Atwood Choral Group

Warden's Comments . . . . M. Hambrick, Warden

Program Coordinator's Comments. . . . . . .M. Whetsell, Coordinator

Recognitions . . . . .M. Whetsell, Coordinator

We're Doing It,
   One Day At A Time . . . . Former Program Participants
            1. Vicki Brooks   2. Tammy Leavoy
            3. Marlee Turner   4. Judy Thain

Emotional Woman . . . . .Choral Reading Group

Closing Remarks . . . . M. Simpson, Regional Drug
                                               Abuse Program Coordinator

We Are The World. . . . . Atwood Choral Group

Benediction . . . . A. Church, Chaplain

Reception and Refreshments

*Ms. Merritt was selected by her peers in the treatment community
to serve as emcee for the 1993 anniversary celebration. She was
chosen for her commitment to recovery and her willingness to
share recovery with others. Ms. Merritt graduated from the
program April 1993.

**Musical accompaniment provided by Nancy Aughey. Choral group
directed by Kim Thomas.

Psychology Services

Certificate of Achievement

This Certifies That

Brenda Merritt

is awarded this Certificate for Successful Completion of the Forty-Hour Drug Education Program Presented at the Federal Medical Center , U.S. Bureau of Prisons, Lexington, Kentucky, this _____26th_____ *day of* _____October_____ *, 1993.*

Becky Brown, M.S.
Drug Treatment Specialist

Mary Whetsell, Ph.D.
Drug Abuse Program Coordinator

Certificate of Recognition

Federal Medical Center
Lexington, Kentucky

Presented to

Brenda Merritt

for

Outstanding Contributions to the Religious Department as:

Member of General Christian Choir

This 19 *day of* June, 19 93

Music Director

Tom Scott, Sr. Chaplain
Chaplain

brenda - remember where you came
from, so you don't go back there! keep
focused forward & upward. good luck
in your ongoing recovery... Gus Benson

UNITED STATES GOVERNMENT

MEMORANDUM
FMC, Lexington, Kentucky

Ms. Merritt,
    you've come a long
way in your recovery.
Never ever Forget the
road you're traveled.
you've got a lot of
Life to "Look forward"
to "one day at a time."
Ms. Brown

DATE: April 30, 1993

REPLY TO
ATTN OF: Michael Di Biasie, Ph.D.
Drug Abuse Program Coordinator

SUBJECT: DRUG TREATMENT COMPLETION

TO: Brenda Merritt
Reg. No. 02310-089

Brenda
Make this the
start of a full
& happy life.
Use what you
have learned
to go out &
achieve the
best for you &
your family.
The path you
choose is yours...
Mrs. Crittondio

Brenda,
You can lead a
positive and clean
life. Work hard and
allow yourself to
achieve your goals.
Mr. Kiser

Brenda,
I have seen
work hard for you
recovery. I hope you
will continue working
you better your life. I
are worth it, life. I
Ms. Long

CONGRATULATIONS! You have successfully completed the
twelve month Pilot Drug Treatment Program. The Atwood
Treatment Staff want to take this opportunity to
acknowledge your accomplishments.

To successfully complete this intensive program you had
to honestly examine all aspects of your life. That
examination took a great deal of willingness and courage.
Upon examination of your life, you found character
defects and weaknesses that needed to be changed. You
then set about the difficult task of changing your
patterns and methods of dealing with various life
situations.

You have demonstrated ability to listen, when you did not
want to hear what was being said. You have learned to be
open and share your past with others, so they may
benefit. You have learned that you have many choices in
life and to choose more wisely.

As you begin the next phase of your journey into
recovery, we hope you will take the tools you have gained
with you, so that you will be able to meet your
challenges as they arise. We have seen growth in many
areas during the past year, continue to learn and grow.
Best of luck in all you choose in your future. Remember
to KEEP IT SIMPLE and take it ONE DAY AT A TIME.

Brenda,
Best of luck in all you choose.
I enjoyed having you in my S&I
class. You've made lots of progress.
carry your message to others,
and remember to work your
program daily.
Buzy Mey

Brenda,
Keep open with your feeling Brenda.
Don't close off. Be grateful for the
blessings you have received. You will
be missed in Safe small group.
Keep humble! Work hard.
Mr. McAdamS

30

Professional Development Certificate
Pipeline to Employment for the Justice Involved

Sponsored by the Department of Workforce Development and the Department of Corrections

THIS CERTIFIES THAT

Brenda Merritt

Has successfully completed the two-week Employment Skills & Job Readiness Curriculum Training, and is therefore awarded this

CERTIFICATE OF COMPLETION

Given this 21st day of October, 2019

Employment & Training Supervisor

Reentry Lead

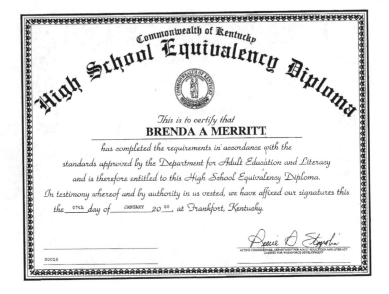

Commonwealth of Kentucky

High School Equivalency Diploma

This is to certify that

BRENDA A MERRITT

has completed the requirements in accordance with the

standards approved by the Department for Adult Education and Literacy

and is therefore entitled to this High School Equivalency Diploma.

In testimony whereof and by authority in us vested, we have affixed our signatures this

the ___07th___ day of ___JANUARY___ 20 _00_, at Frankfort, Kentucky.

ACTING COMMISSIONER, DEPARTMENT FOR ADULT EDUCATION AND LITERACY
CABINET FOR WORKFORCE DEVELOPMENT

00016

32

MEMORANDUM
U.S. GOVERNMENT, DEPARTMENT OF
JUSTICE
Bureau of Prisons
FMC-Lexington, Kentucky

April 1, 1994

TO: Younity Unit Officer

FROM: Christina Benson, Atwood DAT Specialist

RE: Group Attendance

Please allow inmate Brenda Merritt # 02310-089, from Atwood Hall,
to attend the class on sign language offered on Younity Unit on
Monday evenings from 7 to 8 p.m.

If there are any questions, please contact any Atwood staff.

cc: file

Certificate of Achievement

This Certifies that

Brenda Merritt

has completed the

Horizons Inc. Residential Program

Given on October 30, 1995 in Milwaukee, Wisconsin

President – Board of Directors

Executive Director

Program Director

For Equal Economic Opportunity **MILWAUKEE URBAN LEAGUE**
2800 West Wright Street · Milwaukee, Wisconsin 53210 · Phone (414) 374-5850 Fax (414) 562-0249

May 22, 1997

To whom it may concern:

I am writing to you in behalf of Brenda Merritt, a registered client of the Milwaukee Urban League.

As lead worker/Job Developer for the Milwaukee Urban League I have observed Ms. Merritt practice good job readiness skills. Her use of time management skills in relation to keeping appointments and being punctual has/will contribute to her success. Her drive to be dependable, loyal and committed to the tasks at hand all add to a great work ethic.

Moreover, I am satisfied to recommend Ms. Merritt for a position that will match her skill interests. Ms. Merritt has proven to be one of the crown jewels of a very prodigious caseload of clients here at the Milwaukee Urban League. I will be happy to answer any further questions you may have in regards to my client.

Sincerely,

William F. Richardson, Jr.

A United Way Fund Agency · A National Urban League Affiliate

*In Recognition of
the Fulfillment of the Requirements
for Certification*

WISCONSIN

CERTIFICATION BOARD

Hereby Certifies
BRENDA MERRITT

as a

Registered Alcohol Drug Counselor I

02/25/98
Date Awarded
02/25/99
Valid thru _____

President, WCB

Registration No. 11029

High Tech Office Training

Certificate
of
Completion

This is to certify that

Brenda A. Merritt

has satisfactorily completed the Six Week Course of Study
in
High Tech Office Training
specializing in Microsoft Office Programs

Community Enterprises of Greater Milwaukee
3118 North Teutonia Avenue
Milwaukee, Wisconsin

William H. Lock, Executive Director   Henderson Lee Brown, Instructor

Endorsed this Third Day of March of the Year Two-Thousand

PRISON FELLOWSHIP.
Ministries

In recognition of participation in the seminar,

"Steps to Christian Growth"

BRENDA MERRITT

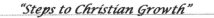

a child of God, is hereby awarded this

Certificate of Participation

"Be strong in the Lord and in his great power. Wear the full armor of God. Wear God's armor so that you can fight against the devil's evil tricks."
Ephesians 6:10-11 New Century Version

_____
Charles W. Colson

_____
Instructor

_____
Chaplain

6 November 2004
Date

(NBTD)

38

PRISON FELLOWSHIP.
Ministries

In recognition of training completed,

Brenda Merritt

is hereby presented this

Diploma

to certify the successful completion of Prison Fellowship's Training, which equips volunteers to offer hope through Jesus Christ to those touched by crime.

Full Certification; In-Prison Ministry

"Do your best to present yourself to God as one approved, a workman who does not need to be ashamed and who correctly handles the word of truth."

2 Timothy 2:15 NIV

_____
Charles W. Colson

_____
Field Director

_____
Pastor

November 15, 2004
Date

"A bruised reed he will not break . . . In faithfulness he will bring forth justice." Isaiah 42:3

INTX0

Institutional Ministries

Sharing hope with those who need it most!

Governor Scott Walker

March 10, 2017, 2017

To Whom it may concern,

My name is Deaconess Sarah Guenther. I have had the privilege of doing ministry in various jails, detention centers, prison, nursing homes and other various institutions in Wisconsin since 1993. Early in my ministry I had an opportunity to meet Ms. Brenda Merritt. Throughout those years I have had the joy of walking with Ms. Merritt through many different seasons of life. I have seen her through losses and joys, struggles and new opportunities. Ms. Merritt has shown me that, through times of stress which inevitably come, that she has developed the skill of developing and using the resources available to her. She has identified wonderful people (professional and friendly) and programs which support her physically, emotionally and spiritually. I believe this ability to discern when she needs help and how to find it is a key to her ability to ride the storms successfully the last fifteen years since I have known her.

Ms. Merritt has many gifts and talents, along with her experience, that can be and have been an inspiration and help to others. I believe that receiving a pardon would open more opportunities for Ms. Merritt to continue to move forward in pursuits consistent with the identity she has from her faith and her most recent and solid successful past.

Thank you for taking the time to read and consider this letter and allowing Ms. Merritt the opportunity to move forward unencumbered from needless labels and restrictions which benefit neither Ms. Merritt nor the community at large.

Sincerely,

Sarah Owens Guenther
Deaconess Wisconsin Lutheran Institutional Ministries

2323 N. Mayfair Rd. #480 Wauwatosa, WI 53226 — 414-259-4370 — www.im.life

Milwaukee

Jobs For Progress, Inc.

Certificate of Completion

Awarded to

BRENDA MERRITT

Recognizing the completion of all requirements in

BASIC CLERICAL SKILLS TRAINING

Awarded
Date of

12/3/01

Executive Director

Gloria Rozanski

Instructor

Certificate of Achievement

This certifies that

BRENDA MERRITT

has successfully completed 14.25 hours of training for the:

ARKANSAS LEADERSHIP ACADEMY

October 19th-21st, 2009

Kathy Muscari Ph.D., Director: Technical Assistance Center

Consumer Organization and
Networking Technical Assistance Center

Certificate of Achievement

This Certifies That

Brenda Merritt

is awarded this certificate for
Completing ___45___ Hours
in the

Parenting Program

On this ___1st___ day of ___July___ 1994

_____
Instructor

_____
Supervisor of Education

BETHEL-BETHANY UNITED CHURCH OF CHRIST
2878 N. 54ᵗʰ Street
2866 N. 54ᵗʰ Street (Office)
Milwaukee, WI 53210

TIMOTHY R. PERKINS, Pastor
Phone: (414) 442-1281
E-mail: perkdrews@aol.com

Friday, June 25, 2004

Dear Prison Fellowship,

I have known Brenda Merritt for several years as her Pastor and friend. During that time, she has been a committed member of our church community and a faithful volunteer at the Cathedral Center Women's Shelter in Milwaukee. Brenda brings a yearning to serve and a compassionate heart that make her a good candidate for volunteer ministry with Prison Fellowship.

Having spent time in prison and knowing the power of God's love to heal and liberate, Brenda has a deep desire to share her faith journey with others. She also benefited greatly from her own experience with Prison Fellowship and is very interested in being part of your important ministry. I hope and pray that you will consider inviting Brenda to serve with you.

Please feel free to call me at 414-442-1281 or Email me at PerkDrews@aol.com., if you have further questions.

God's Peace,

Timothy R. Perkins

Rev. Dr. Timothy R. Perkins

Certificate of Achievement

This certifies that
Brenda Merritt

has successfully completed the
PHOENIX Program
through
The Milwaukee Outreach Center
January 16-19 and 22, 2007

**Providing an opportunity for new
beginnings through
discovering ones significance,
purpose, and direction for LIFE.**

Signature (TMOC) 1/22/2007
Date

Signature (TMOC) 01/22/07
Date

45

Certificate of Completion

This document certifies that

Brenda Merritt

Has successfully completed the following classes during the Spring of 2006

Introduction to Computer Basics
Introduction to Microsoft Word XP
Introduction to Microsoft Excel XP

In Accordance with Interfaith Employment Services Programs.

Patricia Delmenhorst
Director of Employment Services

6647 W. Mill Road • Milwaukee, WI 53218
Phone: (414) 760-0334 • Fax: (414) 760-0399 • www.tmoc.org

May 14, 2007

Brenda Merritt
3405 West 14th Street
Pine Bluff, AR 71603

Dear Brenda,

I appreciated your call on Saturday. I can't completely realize the difficulty that you are
going through at this time; however, I will continue to pray for you.

Thank you again for your work at the resale shop. You were a dedicated worker who did
what was asked and more. You did it well. I have enclosed your final check.

Please stay in touch in any way that you can.

In His service,

Bill Lange

Penetrating Lives for Lasting Change

MENTOR TRAINING

Certificate of Completion

PRESENTED TO

Brenda Merritt

FOR SUCCESSFUL COMPLETION OF
MENTOR BASIC TRAINING

INSTRUCTOR

April 16, 2005

Prison
Fellowship®

Certificate of Achievement

This certifies that

Brenda Merritt

has successfully completed
WINGS Life Skills Training
through The Outreach Foundation &
The Milwaukee Outreach Center
June 5-9, 2000

OUTREACH
FOUNDATION

WINGS
LIFE · SKILLS · TRAINING

The winds have welcomed you with softness. The sun has blessed you with its warmth. You have flown so high and so well that God has joined you in your laughter and sets you gently back into the loving arms of His created Earth. May your skies always be blue, your winds fair and your landings soft.

Signature _____ Date 9-9-00

Signature _____ Date 6-9-2000

49

5. There was a Nun that I had met when I was age seventeen. Back then she invited me to the women's center which was in the neighborhood where I resided. Surprisingly, she came to visit me. It was great to get a visit from her. She was such a supportive person back then. Before our visit was over. She made the shape of a cross on my forehead with her index finger and said a thoughtful, meaningful Prayer. We smiled as we said our good bye. That imprint lies within my head along with the beautiful prayer that she prayed.

However, I'll never forget years later in my life she told me that she couldn't have anything to do with me anymore. And didn't. So, all I could say was: Oh well. She didn't tell me the reason nor did I ask.

There were so many wonderful things that occurred that amazed me, even if they were rude awakenings, I found the spiritual side of them all.

There was also a wellness class within the programs' agenda.

One summer day, some of the members and I were outside walking the track. One of the Counselors and I were slowly walking and talking, when someone came up to speak to her for a minute and I walked over by the grass just glancing at the ground, suddenly I saw a bug walking on the grass that looked just like a tiny little human being. It had 2 legs, 2 arms and a body. Its head looked like a human face. It saw me and stood there with the two arms sorts reaching toward me, as if it wanted me to pick it up. I stared at it with my mouth wide open and went right away to get the Counselor to show her the strange thing that I had seen. She wasn't that far but, when we went back, it was going on under the gate. It looked as though it waved at us. Man! I was like in a state of shock. Though the counselor didn't find it to be strange at all. She said that she sees them on a regular basis. Now that moment followed me for the rest of my life. God knows that it was what it was. It puzzled me more than anything else. Though I just knew God wanted me to see it for whatever reason, so as long as it was created by Him, there were no worries.

Anyways, I thank God for giving me the ability to actually achieve my goals.

There was more. Now on the other hand the negative gossip had to be in the mix, because everybody didn't like me. I had some back stabbers. Just to elaborate on some of those incidents; I used to go to a Parenting class. The instructor was a beautiful young lady. Word was that she was gay. However, she and I became close associates; next word was that we were dating. Which wasn't true. I believe the attraction may have been there, though we never discussed that type of thing. She was just cool like me. We admired one another's style.

Now on the other hand there was one dyke that was strongly attracted to me, but was supposed to respect the fact that we were not on the same page. We said we were cool with one another's preferences. She was all right with that until the prison became co-ed.

I had completed two and a half years of my time. The Wardens and Officials had made a decision to house the men at the prison, that they would slowly start transferring the women out to other available prisons. Until then the prison would be co-ed. It was not surprising when suddenly the majority of the supposed to be gay chicks turned against their dykes. It was the biggest drama scene that I had witnessed while being there. Some of the men were working in the kitchen cooking and serving our food. Whenever we went through the serving line, we would have contact with them. We used to send kites (short letters), money and etc. through that line. It was the first time that I had begun to break the rules. Lol. Because there were two guys that I found to be attractive. One worked on the line, the other one worked at the widow where we dropped our dirty dishes.

One day I was at that window chatting with my guy Trell when all of the sudden the gay chick came from behind me and snatched me from the window, then put me in a head lock. What she didn't know about me was that I was an OG (older gangster), I had grown up fighting and wasn't afraid of anyone. So, it was easy for me to come up out of her hold and push her off of me. My next instinct was to cold cock her dead in her forehead and just do the darn thing until one of my favorites officers came and broke us up. A lot of the chicks had came running out of the dining area to see what was up. But it had quiet down so that no one would go to the hold. I was so embarrassed. I left and went back to the unit.

I heard that the two guys who were interested in me had a confrontation about which one of them did I really belong too. Lol. It was all a big joke. The one named Gee didn't seem as interested as Montrell, though I had met him first and just didn't let Gee go or know. I nicked named him Gee in which mine was Bree Bree.

Later on in that same day I went down to the gym, the first place where I first met ole' girl. She was working out. I went over to the area where I normally work out. She came over to me talking about apologizing, I got up and quietly left, after I gave her that; "don't say nothing to me chick" look. She appeared to be sorry, but sorry wasn't good enough for me. That was basically the end of our communication.

That incident had given Miss. Wonderful the wrong impression. We ended up talking about all that crap which had given me the opportunity to explain to her that things were not what they seemed to be. I even expressed my feelings for God. Even though, I liked the thrill that she had for me. I was starting to be co-dependent on her. But God said: No!

Next thing you know my criminal mind was on blast because I started illegally crocheting plenty of winter hats to sale to the men and ladies in the Prison. Dudes were buying the heck out of them.

I guess all of the sudden Gee wanted to get a profit from my earnings. You know. I was like No, wrong answer dude. I even stopped talking to him on that tip. He was not a playa'! He put me in the mind of this guy who used to be on my case about prostituting, but wanted me to be down for him after he decided to get in that game. Another wrong answer.

So Trell and I did get closer, exchanged personal information. So that we would keep in touch after we were released.

Far as Miss. Wonderful, eventually she was in the first group that was shipped out to a different Prison. We said we would keep in touch, even though we attempted to keep our words, but it wasn't long after the letters had discontinued.

More transfers happened sooner than later. Men and ladies were getting caught making out in different places on a regular basis. That burst all of our bubbles. Lol. All I could say was that it was fun while it lasted. I never was caught.

As time went on, the messier I became. I heard that if we had a medical condition, that a person wouldn't get shipped out until later on. So, I had decided to have a bunionectomy on both feet. The only reason was for me to have the ability to stay at the prison to flirt with Gee and Trell. After the surgery I had to go to the Infirmary just for a few weeks in an order for my feet to heal. The Infirmary was located in the main building where the sick inmates stayed.

I even had a chance to get a few kisses from Gee. After that I started messing around with him again. My mother had sent me a gold chain that I had chosen to give to him. The one that I had promised to give to my daughter. Wasn't I bogus. Around that time, Trell was in the hold.

After a few weeks of being in there I was sent back to the original unit. I was glad because it was sad being around the ladies who were so very old, but had life in Prison. One of the ladies was there because her grandson was caught with plenty cocaine in the trunk of her car, which was registered in her name. She ended up doing the time, sad thing was that no one sent her money or visited her after that matter. Another one was there because she had shot and killed two Sheriffs for trying to arrest her son. No correspond. She was one of the ones that died in that Prison, which completed her life sentence.

There were many more. It wasn't a coincidence that I ended up in that place. Seems like God was allowing me to realize what could possibly happen to me if I were to continue being dishonest and intoxicated. Well, sure enough He caught my attention. Because, my heart was breaking daily as I watched those old ladies being removed from prison to their grave.

CHAPTER 3

The Boulevard where I found God's Peace within myself

January of Nineteen Ninety-Five for the third time the Parole Broad appeared again. Staff had called for my name over the loud speaker to report to the office where the cases were submitted to determine whether an inmate could possibly get an early release. Well, I chose not to even go see them. Just totally ignored the command. So, they packed up their little meaningless papers and left the premises.

However, by the time that I went back to unit my Case Manager put me in check about refusing the call. Well hell, I told him that I was devastated after being turned down twice by that ridiculous Parole Board staff.

However, to my surprise my Case Manager told me that my release date had dropped. I was to be released ten days before my original release date. Which was great by me. Joy went through my whole body. I was so happy to hear that news. Now I hadn't bothered my mom much at all through the years of my incarceration. But suddenly I kept calling her at least three times every day until I left. We were so happy. It was great to have the ability to start planning all that I was going to do.

Words can't express how wonderful and relieved I was. After preparing myself to go home, I had given things away, such as my clothes and other personals things that I could buy at home. Said a lot of good byes. Everyone was talking about the beautiful glow I had about myself, well hell I couldn't stop smiling or sleep much. I was being the happiest person in the whole wide world. Chills would go up and down my spine when I thought about seeing my 4 Angels. My daughter, I had written a dairy that I wanted to give to her. I couldn't wait to share it with her. Lord what a blessing you had given to me.

The day that I was released I went to pick up my money that they owed me. It was like three hundred dollars. I called a cab. When the cab came, I stood there crying tears of joy, waving bye to all my cell mates.

However, after getting into the back seat of the cab. I didn't look back.

We headed straight for the Greyhound Bus Station. Upon our arrival I found out what time the bus would leave, which had given me enough time to go across the street to a Dollar General Store.

Brenda A Merritt

I was so out done when I ran into one of the male counselors (from the Prison) who believed in my success big time. We were not allowed to hug the men at the Prison, but he sure gave me a big one at that store. I'll never forget how impressed I was. He was actually breaking the rules. However, trusting and knowing that he could put his job at risk without having any complications is what blew me back. Not that it made his decision right or wrong, at that time it was all about me and I felt good about it and didn't say a word. That was all I'm saying. He bought me a 3-piece McDonald's magnet set for my refrigerator. The set is still on there as I write. He asked me to promise that if I ever felt like using, that I'll go look on my refrigerator to remind me of where I came from. We said our good byes and I went to catch my bus. I was thinking to myself how he probably couldn't wait to hug on my big breast. LOL

but seriously, surely, he was tempted as well as many of those Officers. Most important he waited.

I never tempted any of the officers. Instead, I encouraged some of them to think about the consequences of a temporarily feeling.

A boarding the bus.

There weren't many people on it at all, so I had taken advantage of that and set right up front by the driver and talked until I couldn't talk anymore. Lol. It was so hilarious; I was talking so fast, using run on sentences and all. That bus driver kept saying; "Well Thank God, you made it through those 3 years, because a lot of us couldn't have done that much time." I told him; "You know what bus driver, I've learned that we can do anything that we put our minds to, that I'm a child of God"!

Finally, I relaxed a little and started thinking about what a wonderful day it was for me, it was one of the best days in my life.

There were a few layovers before we entered into Milwaukee.

For one City in particular was Cincinatti. It was so damn gorgeous downtown, just absolutely marvelous had I known better I'd thought I was in Las Vegas. Taking a trip with my children to both of those cities were on my bucket list.

Just riding through there put so many positive things on my heart.

There may not have been a whole lot of good memories, but Thank God there were many possibilities and opportunities in my future plans.

I had also Thanked God for giving me the ability to actually achieve my goals.

The bus arrived in Milwaukee at 6 in the morning. I was slow getting off because I had my 4 bags with a lot of personal priceless things that I just couldn't leave with anyone. Plus, I had went shopping at that Store back in Lex. Finally, a guy helped me with at least getting those tote bags off the top shelf of the bus.

The closer I got to the front of the bus the more I could clearly see all of my immediate family members and two of our close friends were standing on the side walk by the bus stop, which was in the garage of Greyhound station. There they all were my four children, mom, two sisters, four brothers, two nephews, three nieces, and two very close friends of our family!!! I was like, OH my, I couldn't take it. One of my brothers had his camcorder, filming everything that was going on. He had taken a break to hug me and tease me about getting some gum. Because I had mention to him when I was still in the prison that we couldn't have any, so we were all hugging and laughing, I was so glad to be back in my hometown in a pleasant occasion

with all of us, that was one of the days to always remember and cherish for the rest of my life. I have a copy of the film. Being that the time that I would have to check into the Halfway House wasn't until later, we all decided to go to Mickey Ds to have breakfast. Yes, it was the same House.

After we completed our meal, we all went to the place which seemed to be my home away from home. I would live for six months. My Guardian Angel, Barb who was expecting me, greeted us all in. We all hugged, laughed and talked for a while until they all left. First, we made arrangements to meet again. It was all good, though I hated to see them go.

Knowing that they would return soon had given me a lot of hope. It wouldn't be long before we would reunite again. I had to keep reminding myself of that.

I was assigned to the same Counselor that I had prior to that present time. I didn't know rather to like her or not. My decision was to go ahead to accept my responsibility for my actions; too trip as less as possible.

At that time, I realized that I had relapsed (start thinking the same old things) in my mind before leaving the Prison. Ideas that I acted on knowingly they never worked for me, but I expected different results??? However, by attending a Relapse Prevention class in the program, helped me to remember the effective coping skills that I learned and the main thing was I needed to continue to allow God's solution be a part of my every decision, as quick as I could. Some of those times I made better decisions than other times. However, I needed to be alright with everything. Right or wrong. I said; "So what". I'm a fallible human learning how this thing works. I just gave it my best shot.

You know … at that time in my life I had come back down to earth, three years clean time from drugs and alcohol, 2 of those years. I had been saved, without having a lot of knowledge of what all that meant but I just believed in Jesus and had faith at such a time like then. That was all I needed. Everything else fell into place. All my needs were being met.

Day one: Barb and I had gone to her office to update my records and to chat about my experience at the Prison. After that I went to my room, unlocked the door with a key, I felt so funny inside, as if I was doing something wrong. Then I unpacked and decorated my side of the room. I just couldn't be still. Right away I started filling out the enrollment papers that Barb had given to me. It was all kinds of excitement. A lot of the ladies that I knew were coming to say hey. I met my roommate for the first time, come to find out she wanted to be more than that to me. But of course, I wasn't down like that. So, she respected me in a sense. A lot of times I found myself talking to her about how different we were and how ok it was with me. There wasn't a desire for me to judge her nor anyone else as far as that was, no one had did any worse than what I had done. Come on now. Let's keep it real. I wasn't knocking her. For another thing I didn't have time to try to keep up with her life.

My children had started coming over and were able to spend the nights. Wow, it was a dream comes true. We did many activities together as a family. Everything went well the whole time that I was there. in myself, like unbelievable. I couldn't take it. She was

I met my new parole officer; she was God sent! For real. Man, she had seen some things in me that I did not see very spiritual and religious and amazing. Put me in the mind of an Angel.

My first day out I went by my mom house where everybody was it was so noisy and a lot was going on until I just couldn't cope with being over there. The children were there laughing and having fun with one another. My mom was cooking. She was listening to Gospel music in one room. I was playing inappropriate music. Anytime Anyplace by: J. Jackson. In a different room. I was not used to kicking it like that. it seemed to be a bit much.

Thank God my nephew told my eldest son to bring it to my attention about the music that I was listening to. I felt so embarrassed to the point that I asked someone to take me back. My mom was sorry that I wanted to go back sooner than expected. But she understood I just wasn't fitting in. First mistake. I felt uncomfortable, paranoid and out of place. I felt better after I was dropped off back to the Halfway House. Barb had asked me why was I back so early. After I explained. She said that what I went through was normal for someone who had been down for so long.

As time went on, I was able to go job searching. Urban League had an employment program. I met another Angel. He was my Job Coach. After telling him a lot of my back ground, he understood that just maybe I deserved another chance. So, he made it his business to get me a job.

I was hired at a place where we processed pharmaceutical merchandise. It was cool. I enjoyed working there. Ended up working there off and on for 7 years. The job was a blessing. Plus, the Coach was a Pastor and used to pray with me, unlike a lot of people in a leadership position. Sad to say, but especially our African American people. We seem to take our position for granted and start power thrusting. I become sad it when I see that situation happening.

The resident of the Halfway House voted for me to be the President of the affairs. I was very excited about it and did do a damn good job as their leader.

CHAPTER 4

The Parkway Where I Met Resilience

Another blessing.

My Parole Officer was so proud of me. She was in fact watching all of my positive attributes and as a result was making plans to Bless me even more so.

Doing that time my parole officer was seriously helping me become very productive. I may have started out kind of fearful but I did get in the groove. Especially after meeting more positive people who believed in me. That made a big difference. I also started going to outside meetings, where there were many other recovering people. Those meetings were not what I was truly interested in; for one thing it was too much going on that was not true recovery stuff. Phone numbers were passed from person to person as if it was the dating game. It was called the thirteenth step. The step where we started defocusing on self and yet instead would give our undivided attention to anyone else.

It wasn't that I didn't like relationships, it was just something that I knew I wasn't ready for. And I didn't hook up with anyone until 9 months later.

It was long after when I had chosen to discontinue going to the meeting places. The only reason that I attended as long as I did was because it was a requirement. My Parole Officer allowed my choice to be granted.

There was a Fifteen-Hundred-dollar restitution fee that went along with my sentencing. In which I was able to make payments regularly. After paying so much my Parole Officer (who was pregnant back then) requested an order that the balance would be eliminated and just like I thought she won and I was able to continue to save money for my 3-bedroom house that I was about to accomplish sooner than later. Which would enable me to have my family back together.

ALREADY!

I had to purchase the necessaries for us to live safely. They were not court ordered out of my custody or anything; so yes, I just needed to obtain the proper furniture.

It was another great day to Graduate from the Halfway House.

It was my pleasure. I packed my things and headed for my mother's house. That was the place where I would live until I found the house along with the proper furnishers.

Two weeks later we moved from my mom's house. We moved into a nice 3 bedroom on Sixty seventh West Keefe Parkway (PKWY). It was beautiful. All I could say was: Look at God.

I had met 2 friendly Christian ladies who came from a certain Ministry. People who supported the single parents who had children. They were in fact very helpful and we are continuing to be friends. My support person was Sand. Right to this day I love her dearly.

They were more Angels added to my list.

My children and I didn't attend a Church right away, which was one of my goals. Though, we had discussions concerning God a lot. We prayed over our food and said night time prayers as well. though that wasn't enough for me. There was a Church out there just calling my name.

Around this time, there were many men interested in me. I didn't give in to them though. It was to my surprise that even after I ran into my X man. Goo Goo, a guy that I was so infatuated with. I let him know that my priority was basically about building a healthy relationship on my children. Therefore, he eventually saw that we still did not work out. I didn't want any commitments to him because unlike me, I realized that he wasn't ready to settle down yet, though, I did want him. At that time. I had learned about the difference between a want and need.

My job was going pretty well. Things were starting to get better. My Parole Officer wasn't visiting that much nor was she scheduling me to go see her that often. It was all good.

My children and I were getting along great but I noticed my baby boy were experiencing some hardships at school. There was a concern. My mom had mentioned that he had been acting out at school and at home, while I was away.

It had come to the point of me missing several days from work. Then I became very concerned. Not only about my son but also the job. Well by the Grace of God everything was put in the proper manner. My son was going to be all right and my job was not a concern any more, at that perfect time. In the mean while between time everything was going in my favor.

It became time for The Urban League program to maintain a fundraising function. By God's Grace I was chosen as the most successful single parents in the particular class in which I was enrolled. Along with a majority of other selected students that were involved in different classes of the Program. That choice consisted of me going to the Bradley Center to have some photo shoots made where I had six different possess.

Another blessing.

After that I was led to go to V 100 a radio station here in Milwaukee. Where they recorded my story about how Urban League had helped me while I was in the Program. I also mentioned how they had helped my eldest son, Michael as well. My Counselor had given me more information about the Fund-Raising Celebration called The Black and White Ball for many different Projects in the Community to gather together to express how they are supporting the people who were in need of second chances.

One of the best pictures will be blown up to a 7 by 7 ft. black and white photo. That a light would shine on each photo individually as their voice would begin to tell their success story. After the show was over, Urban League showed their appreciation by giving and delivering our extra-large portrait to us. What a wonderful thing to have had the opportunity to part take therein.

Man, I was just thinking about how Blessed I was for doing the right thing, which encouraged me to just continue to do the darn thing at any given time. One day at a time.

Eventually, we moved from Sixty fourth west Keefe to Seventy Sixth in Silver Spring Drive. Again, that house was a beautiful 3 bedroom lower flat. However, the second day of living there someone had broken into our house and stole some toys and a few other expensive things such as a sack of fourteen karat gold jewelry.

After realizing how I had left the window in my bedroom cracked. I made sure to double check everything before leaving for work. From that after there were not any more robberies. Ok, so time went on I started to realize why I chose to run from reality and try to yet instead suppress all my problems away by drinking alcohol until I would become completely drunken out of this world. Sometimes I still find myself thinking; No wonder I was drunk. My life was just a hard knock life. No baby daddies around to help a sister out. The guys that I met just wouldn't do either, so there I went playing the role of a mother, father and without a husband. However, because of who I had become in Christ, All things were possible through Christ who had in fact strengthen me. A wrench like me. I made it by praying, laughing and keeping God alive in everything I did. Utilizing all the tools of maintaining sobriety. Being resilient in my way.

Becoming a member of C.F.F. Church also encouraged me to keep positive motivating forces within my life. It was such a very gracious Church when we first started going there. Newly built. The Pastor was one of best Preachers around town. I learned a lot.

I saw the Church grow from one hundred to a thousand members in a matter of weeks.

I moved on after there was too much going on there. To this day I don't have any regrets. Glory to God.

So, life went on and we started going to The Word of God Church. I used to pay my tithes regularly. However, in 2002 I decided to buy a brand-new Chevy. And was unable to pay my tithes. I seriously didn't know if that was well with the Lord, so I had taken my concern to the Minister, where I still didn't get an answer to my concern. I started feeling uncomfortable and left the Church.

I really didn't understand what was going on at the Churches, all I knew was something that I didn't understand. After a while I had started changing Churches just as much as I was moving from house to house.

CHAPTER 5

The Parkway Where I Met Resilience

Throughout the years I remained clean and sober. Dealt with my life to the best of my ability. Perhaps, it seems like I'm stuck on this particular Avenue. But, God says that I am not at the end of my road.

I was able to become a positive role model for my children who I adore and will forever adore the most. I was able to be the best Aunt to many of my nephews and nieces.

There I was, loving everything that God had chosen to do in my life. For me, being part of the solution was a major priority to me. I allowed God to take the steering wheel and guide and lead me in His directions. Which were so right and satisfying to my soul. Lord has Mercy. I was so Blessed. I mean I experienced what it truly meant in the Bible about how God would pour out so many Blessings where you won't have room for any more. I used to think that it meant a money or material thing. But I realized that He was talking about running our cup over with unexplainable, priceless, wonderful and great spiritual beings. God talks to me and show me unimaginable things on a daily basis. Yes, so be careful what you ask for because you just might get it. Be careful and make sure that you can handle the truth. It may take a while but it will eventually set you free.

Roll with all those uncomfortable feelings, for they are forever changing. Do what you know is best for you and yours.

As I close this book but never the thoughts within. Stay tuned for my upcoming books. For I have decided to write for the rest of my life.

May God's Speed be with you forever.

Keep an open mind and allow His Grace to fade you in all things. My last Avenue will be on a road down south in Sheridan. The place where I found my safe haven.

You'll see that He's real and the beginning and the end of us all. When so ever we get through. Haven on this broken land. The place where I found Jesus. I was 5 years old.

See you on the other side. There's a gate called Beautiful.

I have been saved for 29 years, without any new criminal cases, no addictions, and I love my four children with love from above.

I pray that this book will be the beginning of the way that I can express my innocence.

To Share my testimony through whatever shape. form or fashion is available for me.

First giving honor and glory to God. thank you, Lord, for saving me through out all the days of my life. Not sure why you did it, but I know this much is true. It was your will, not mine. so here I am again Lord. I'm coming as correct as I can at such a time like this. Words are unable to express my gratitude to You, oh Lord. but I ask you on this day to help me by giving me wisdom to complete your calling. Yes, I have faith that you will do all that I ask of you. My faith can be as small as a mustard seed.

It's faith.

Each day is A New Beginning for me. As I pray my way through, sometimes one minute at a time. Soon and very soon, God will come through. I will become your author of many books. For I am seriously becoming a resilient woman of God. But forever Your Child.

If you are struggling with abuse from mental illness or for whatever reason and you feel lost and turned out all wrong. Prayer is forever a way maker. Talk to God as if He is sitting in front of you in person, surrender all of your fault's day after day, if you need too.

Start loving yourself first readers. Take off the mask that will forever keep you stuck in your negative ways.

Today I am as happy as I can be in this time of my life. I've come to realize how my purpose in life is but only to help others. There are unspeakable blessings for us that will come naturally as a result. From God. have patience and allow Him to do a great work in you.

My future plans are to continue to write my testimony until my last days. My love for others is priceless, I truly care.

Be mindful that this book is only the beginning. The best is yet to come for all of us who Love God and His order. Stay woke. Know that prison is not only behind locked gates and walls. It lies within our soul. We can only shift that bondage in a matter of God's time, speaking to our spirituality and having a living relationship with God.

Finally, accept the fact we are all unique in our own way, nothing more, nothing less.

I made it my business to get a close relationship with my mother, after all the broken years of my life.

When she passed. God told me in His soft voice: "Dear child, don't worry about the loss of your mother, for I give you her heart, it is priceless." Then that statement took the cake and ate it all,

Because, before and after my mother passed. I left to go back to Milwaukee after her funeral.

I felt numbness throughout my body. I was in a state of shock. After praying repeatedly. God's same message came coming to pass. I was able to feel the presence of my mom resting peacefully somewhere, I absolutely love my mom; she is my angel circling around me through-out the entire day. She is the reason that I smile.

Yes there are many things that I can express, however remember, please hear what I am not saying. What I want to say. But, for God's sake I cannot say. But what I will say on His time.

Like I said, I am incredibly happy. However, my reputation is a mess. I do not feel much love from many used to be friends nor my children. Except a few. But I do feel God working a miracle in my entire family's life. Soon, all will be put together in a sense of genuine love. One for the other, Evil will lose its place in our lives. There will not be anymore. None that will keep trouble in our way.

I am speaking it into existence.

When times get hard and unbearable, I can think about having an organism with my brain by relapsing on a drug. Or choose to remember God's power that resides in my higher self.

I will not go back, says the Lord.

Thank you for resilience. I am tying one more knot to pull me through. Please chose to do the same. Do not give up.

I refuse to.

Printed in the United States
by Baker & Taylor Publisher Services